D1285039

Performance Notes by
Adam Perlmutter

ISBN: 978-1-4584-1093-1

HAL•LEONARD®
CORPORATION
7777 W. BLUEMOUND RD. P.O. BOX 13819 MILWAUKEE, WI 53213

Visit Hal Leonard Online at
www.halleonard.com

Table of Contents

Introduction

Welcome to *Piano Play-Along For Dummies*. Here, you'll find a wonderful collection of songs in a range of styles — everything from rock 'n' roll classics like Elvis Presley's "Don't Be Cruel," to country favorites like "Walk the Line," to music from the movies like "The Pink Panther." Included with this collection is a pair of CDs containing two versions of each song, one featuring a full arrangement with the piano part as notated in the sheet music so that you can hear exactly how this part should sound, and the other without the piano part so that you can play along with the arrangement as the soloist. Also included are performance notes to guide you in learning the songs, along with a bit of trivia for each song. Enjoy!

About This Book

For each song, I include a bit of background information to satisfy the historically curious. This information is followed by a variety of tidbits that struck me as I made my way through the teaching of these songs, including some of the following:

✔ A run-down of the parts you need to know.

✔ A breakdown of some of the chord progressions important to playing the song effectively.

✔ Some of the critical information you need to navigate the sheet music.

✔ Some tips and shortcuts you can use to expedite the learning process.

In many cases, you may already know how to do a lot of this. If so, feel free to skip over those familiar bits.

How to Use This Book

The music contains vocal and piano parts and guitar frames for each song. And, included throughout are handy performance notes to help you learn how to play these songs and understand how they work. I recommend that you first play through the song, and then practice all the main sections and chords. From there, you can add the tricks and treats of each one — and there are many. Approach each song one section at a time and then assemble the sections together in a sequence. This technique helps to provide you with a greater understanding of how the song is structured, and enables you to play it through more quickly.

Two CD recordings are included, to let you play along as the soloist. There are two tracks for each song; the first includes the piano part exactly as it's written in the sheet music. Use this track for listening and study. The second track is the accompaniment only. Play along with this track as the soloist! Both tracks feature Amazing Slow-Downer technology that allows you to change the tempo as you practice.

In order to follow the music and my performance notes, you need a basic understanding of scales and chords. But if you're not a wiz, don't worry. Just spend a little time with the nifty tome *Music Theory For Dummies* by Michael Pilhofer and Holly Day (Wiley), and with a little practice, you'll be on your way to entertaining family and friends.

Conventions Used in This Book

As you might expect, I use quite a few musical terms in this book. Some of these may be unfamiliar to you, so here are a few right off the bat that can help your understanding of basic playing principles:

- **Arpeggio:** Playing the notes of a chord one at a time rather than all together.

- **Bridge:** Part of the song that is different from the verse and the chorus, providing variety and connecting the other parts of the song to each other.

- **Coda:** The section at the end of a song, which is sometimes labeled with the word "coda."

- **Chorus:** The part of the song that is the same each time through, usually the most familiar section.

- **Hook:** A familiar, accessible, or sing-along melody, lick, or other section of the song.

- **Verse:** The part of the song that tells the story; each verse has different lyrics, and each song generally has between two and four of these.

Icons Used in This Book

In the margins of this book are several handy icons to help make following the performance notes easier:

A reason to stop and review advice that can prevent personal injury to your fingers, your brain, or your ego.

These are optional parts, or alternate approaches that those who'd like to find their way through the song with a distinctive flair can take. Often these are slightly more challenging routes, but encouraged nonetheless, because there's nothing like a good challenge!

This is where you will find notes about specific musical concepts that are relevant but confusing to non-musical types — stuff that you wouldn't bring up, say, at a frat party or at your kid's soccer game.

You get lots of these tips, because the more playing suggestions we can offer, the better you'll play. And isn't that what it's all about?

All My Loving

Words and Music by
John Lennon and Paul McCartney

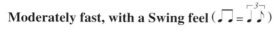

Don't Be Cruel (To a Heart That's True)

Words and Music by
Otis Blackwell and Elvis Presley

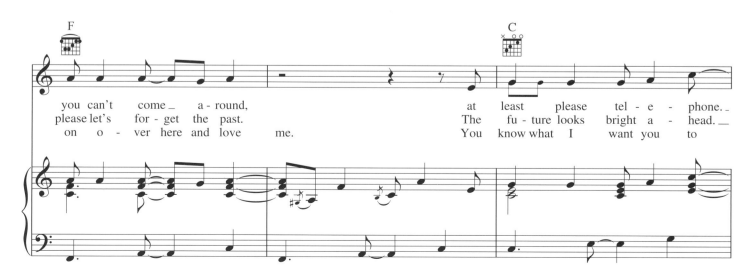

Come What May

Words and Music by
David Baerwald

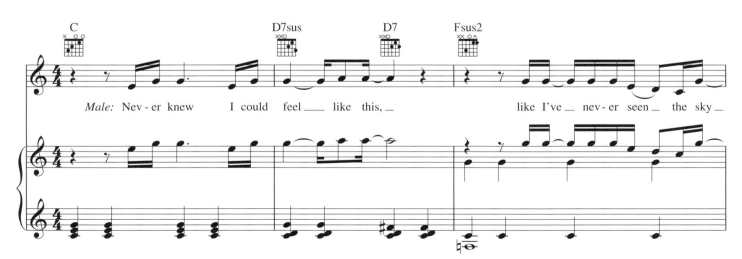

Male: Nev‑er knew I could feel___ like this,___ like I've___ nev‑er seen___ the sky___

God Bless the U.S.A.

Words and Music by
Lee Greenwood

Slowly

If to-mor-row all the things were gone I'd

worked for all my life and I had to start __ a-gain _____ with just my

chil-dren and my wife, I'd thank my luck-y stars ___ to be

I'll Be There

Words and Music by Berry Gordy, Hal Davis,
Willie Hutch and Bob West

You and I must make a pact;
Let me fill your heart with joy and laugh - ter.

we must bring sal - va - tion back.
To - geth - er - ness, well, it's all I'm af - ter.

Where there is love, I'll be there.
When - ev - er you need me, I'll be there.

I Walk the Line

Words and Music by
John R. Cash

Additional Lyrics

3. As sure as night is dark and day is light,
   I keep you on my mind both day and night.
   And happiness I've known proves that it's right.
   Because you're mine I walk the line.

4. You've got a way to keep me on your side.
   You give me cause for love that I can't hide.
   For you I know I'd even try to turn the tide.
   Because you're mine I walk the line.

5. I keep a close watch on this heart of mine.
   I keep my eyes wide open all the time.
   I keep the ends out for the tie that binds.
   Because you're mine I walk the line.

Michelle

Words and Music by
John Lennon and Paul McCartney

semble.   And   I   will   say   the   on - ly   words ____ I   know   that

you'll   un - der - stand   my   Mi - chelle.

Repeat and Fade

Mrs. Robinson

from THE GRADUATE
Words and Music by Paul Simon

Moderately Bright

And here's to you, ___ Mis-sus Rob - in - son, ___ Je - sus loves you more ___

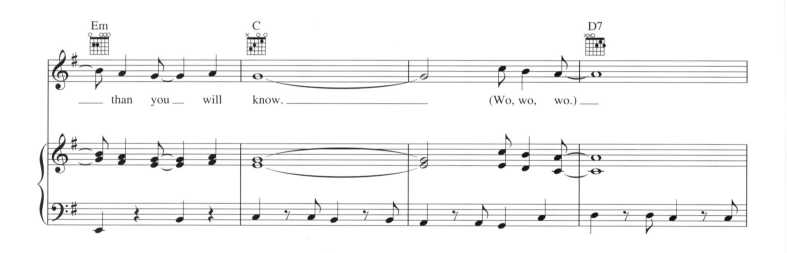

___ than you ___ will know. _____ (Wo, wo, wo.) ___

God bless you, please, Mis-sus Rob - in - son, ___

My Heart Will Go On (Love Theme from 'Titanic')

from the Paramount and Twentieth Century Fox Motion Picture TITANIC
Music by James Horner
Lyric by Will Jennings

CD 1
TRACK
17/18

Moderately

Kansas City

Words and Music by Jerry Leiber and Mike Stoller

Medium Blues

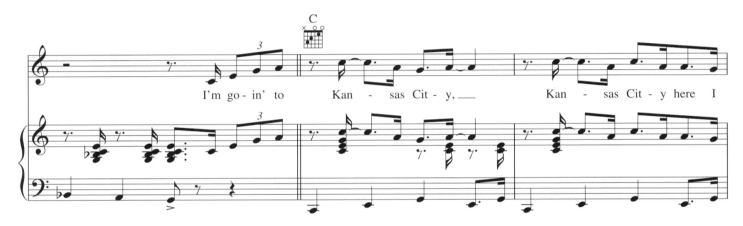

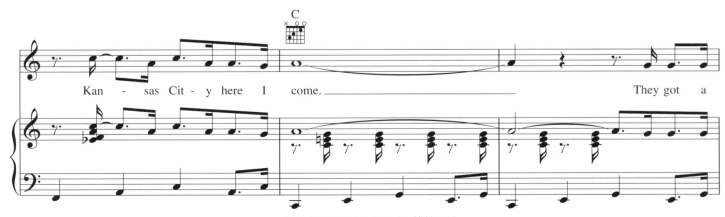

cra - zy way of lov - in' there and I'm gon - na get me some.

I'm go - in' to

They got a cra - zy way of lov - in' there and

I'm gon - na get me some.

Performance Notes

All My Loving (page 5)

Although Paul McCartney normally composed music before lyrics, the words came first with "All My Loving," which he started writing while shaving. McCartney originally conceived of the song as a country western number, but The Beatles recorded it in 1963 in a more decidedly British pop setting. Although it wasn't initially released in the U.S. as a single, "All My Loving" was one of the songs that helped The Beatles gain immense popularity here when they played it on their famous *The Ed Sullivan Show* debut (February 9, 1964).

Written in the key of E major, "All My Loving" is played with a *swing* feel — a rhythm commonly seen in blues, jazz, and other soulful idioms. To achieve a swing feel, wherever you see a pair of eighth notes, play the first note longer than the second (at about a 2:1 ratio between the two notes). It's almost like you're playing a dotted eighth note followed by a 16th note. But be sure not to play these rhythms in a mechanical way.

Come What May (page 13)

In *Macbeth,* William Shakespeare used the phrase "come what may" to mean something like "whatever will be will be." More recently, "Come What May" (not to be confused with the 1952 popular song of the same name) is the name of the love theme sung by Nicole Kidman and Ewan McGregor in the Baz Luhrmann musical film *Moulin Rouge!* Cleverly, "Come What May" is a vehicle for this pair of forbidden lovers to express their amorous feelings for each other. With its gentle syncopation and lovely melody, this song is highly satisfying to play along with on the piano.

Have fun with the syncopated rhythm in the introduction. Be on your toes for the time signature change, from 4/4 to 2/4, in bar nine. As long as you lock in with the accompaniment part, you should be fine, but if you find yourself stumbling, play without the CD until you feel rhythmically confident, then try playing along again.

Don't Be Cruel (To a Heart That's True) (page 8)

One of Elvis Presley's biggest hits, the #1 song "Don't Be Cruel (To a Heart That's True)" was released in 1956 and earned the special distinction of being the only single in recorded history with a B-side ("Hound Dog") that also went to #1. "Don't Be Cruel" was written by Otis Blackwell, a singer/songwriter/pianist whose own recordings never cracked the Top 40, but whose songs for Presley, Jerry Lee Lewis, and others sold millions, creating a template for the new sound known as rock 'n' roll. Though the piano is in the background on the original recording of "Don't Be Cruel," it's in the spotlight for this fun play-along.

Originally played in the key of D major, "Don't Be Cruel" is arranged here in C. One interesting thing about this rock 'n' roll arrangement is the preponderance of *grace notes* that appear throughout, as seen in each small eighth note with a hash mark bisecting the flag and the stem. In many cases, these grace notes are *blue notes,* a minor third in a major key, which lend a soulful quality to the music. As you'll hear on the demo, play each grace note slightly before the full-sized note or notes it precedes, and try to be smooth about it. Be careful not to drop the beat, which is moderately fast and full of swagger.

God Bless the U.S.A. (page 20)

When country musician Lee Greenwood released this heartfelt tribute to America in 1984, it did well, hitting #7 on the country chart. The song continues to be popular, gaining even greater acclaim through the years. Greenwood has described it as, "a song for life and hope, and then, after 9/11, it was a song of unity and rebuilding." Enjoy playing along with the infectious instrumental on the accompaniment track.

"God Bless the U.S.A." has all kinds of sixteenth-note syncopations that if not properly acknowledged, could cause the song to fall apart. If you find yourself struggling to play along with the recording, don't fret, just turn off the CD and *subdivide*. Instead of counting in quarter notes, count, "One-ee-and-uh, two-ee-and-uh, three-ee-and-uh, four-ee-and-uh," and so on. If you learn these rhythms slowly and thoroughly, the next time you see them in a piece of music you'll be able to play them confidently.

I Walk the Line (page 30)

Although many country numbers are all about heartbreak and deceit, "I Walk the Line" is a song of romantic devotion. Johnny Cash wrote the tune in 1956, when he was newly married. He first recorded the song that same year and would record it four more times during his career. The song is regarded as one of Cash's finest, and in fact, according to *Rolling Stone* magazine, one of the 500 Greatest Songs of all Time. There isn't a piano to be found on the original recording of "I Walk the Line," but it sure does work well in this arrangement.

"I Walk the Line" is shown here in the key of F major. It's in *cut time,* as indicated by the time signature, a "C" with a vertical line through it. Feel this meter by counting in half notes, two per bar, rather than quarter notes. If you're following along on the CD, the first two clicks represent two full measures and the clicks that follow are half notes, bringing you in on the pick-up notes. Strive for a bouncing feel throughout; focus on the guitar and bass on the play-along, maybe even imagining a freight train chugging along.

I'll Be There (page 25)

With hits like "I Want You Back" and "ABC," the Jackson 5 were known for their upbeat pop. But the Motown group scored a big hit with the gentle ballad, "I'll Be There," released as a single in 1970. This song proved to be the most successful song ever released by the Jackson 5 and featured Michael Jackson sounding many years older than his tender age of 12. His brother Jermaine was in fine form as well. At the heart of "I'll Be There" is a rather soulful harpsichord, and this part features prominently in our play-along.

If you scan through the music of "I'll Be There" and listen to the CD, you'll see and hear plenty of *quarter-note triplets*. This rhythm is simply three quarter notes in the space usually taken up by two, indicated with a bracketed 3. If you have trouble with it, try counting eighth note triplets on each beat: "trip-uh-let, trip-uh-let," and so on. Listening to the piano on the CD will also help you feel the rhythm. Make sure that you can feel and play quarter-note triplets with accuracy before attempting to master the play-along track.

Kansas City (page 48)

The hard-swinging jazz that percolated in Kansas City during the 1930s is the inspiration for the Jerry Leiber and Mike Stoller song named after this great Midwestern town. The song was first recorded in 1952 by the R&B singer Little Willie Littlefield; seven years later the R&B singer Wilbert Harrison and the rocker Little Richard would have hits with it. You'll be sure to find "Kansas City" with its easy, swinging beat all kinds of fun to play along with.

"Kansas City" is built on the classic *12-bar blues* form, which toggles between the I (C), IV (F), and V7 (G7) chords. This means that once you've learned the first vocal section (bars 5-16) you've essentially learned the whole thing! The bass line is what really makes the song, so try learning the left hand before playing both hands together. Another thing to keep in mind is that this song should really *swing*. In a swing feel, a pair of consecutive eighth notes is played long-short, approximated in the dotted eighth-sixteenth note rhythms that occur throughout. To understand this feel, it's important to do lots of listening. Of course, check out the play-along, and also go straight to the source: any recordings of the Count Basie Orchestra.

Michelle (page 32)

Before he was a Beatle, John Lennon was an art school student. He would take his mates Paul McCartney and George Harrison to parties where revelers dressed in black turtlenecks affected a sophisticated French style that the young musicians found curious. Years later the Beatles would channel their fascination with the French into a ballad called "Michelle," their only song with lyrics in that language. Although the original recording is guitar-driven, it actually works out rather nicely on the piano as you'll see here.

Before jamming along with the play-along to "Michelle," take a moment to enjoy the song's sophisticated harmonies — chords like Fm7 (F–A♭–C–E♭) and Fm6 (F–A♭–C–D). These chords are heard more commonly in jazz than in pop, and help to lend a French flavor to the tune. Here's something cool: *chromatically descending* lines (moving down in half steps) are sometimes used to connect the chords. For instance, in the first four bars of the treble clef, the lowest notes are F, E, E♭, D, D♭, and C in the right hand. Scan through the music to see if you can find other instances of this device at play.

Mrs. Robinson (page 36)

In the 1967 motion picture *The Graduate,* an older, married woman named Mrs. Robinson famously seduces a recent college graduate. The film's director, Mike Nichols, was a huge fan of the singer-songwriter duo Simon & Garfunkel, and he felt their music would evoke the sound he had in mind, so he approached Simon to write some songs for the soundtrack. Simon, who had his own hectic schedule to attend to, ended up missing his deadline. So, he played Nichols a nostalgic song he'd been working on outside of the movie about one Mrs. Roosevelt and Joe DiMaggio. Nichols had Simon change Roosevelt to Robinson, and the movie's theme song, also one of Simon & Garfunkel's greatest hits, was born.

"Mrs. Robinson" is played here in G major in cut time — remember to count two half notes per bar rather than four quarters. This piano arrangement asks the left hand to mimic the bass guitar on the original recording while the right hand, with its two-part harmonies, represents the voices of Simon and Garfunkel. To truly appreciate each part, it would be best to learn this song piece by piece. First tackle the bass line, and for the proper groove be sure to observe the rests. Then, work on the melody, found in the higher notes of the treble clef. Play through the lower notes of the treble clef, in thirds and sixths below, before combining everything and playing along with the recording.

My Heart Will Go On (Love Theme from 'Titanic') *(page 42)*

Sung by Celine Dion, "My Heart Will Go On" is the theme song from the 1997 blockbuster *Titanic* and one of the most popular movie themes of all time. But the song almost didn't make it, because after Dion heard the original demo she didn't want to record it. Her manager and husband, René Angélil, saw the tune's potential, prevailed, and it became not only Dion's biggest hit but one of the best-selling singles in recorded history, selling more than 15 million copies. With its gently rolling arpeggios, this moving song is ideally suited to a piano arrangement.

Arranged here in C♯ minor, "My Heart Will Go On" is multilayered, so just as you did with "Mrs. Robinson," you might try learning the individual parts before tackling the music as a whole. Start by isolating the up-stemmed notes of the treble clef; this is where most of the melody will be found. Next, focus on the down-stemmed notes, where the tied notes provide a distinctive syncopation throughout. Work on the left hand part alone. When you combine all three parts, be sure to play as smoothly and expressively as possible — this is a very sentimental song — and listen carefully as you pedal, so that the notes of the arpeggios ring together. When you think you're ready, reward yourself for your hard work by having a go at the play-along.

The Pink Panther *(page 60)*

Few movie themes have proven as successful both with children and adults as "The Pink Panther" from the 1963 film of the same name. Henry Mancini's instrumental number was released the following year as a single, where it went all the way to the Top 10 on *Billboard*'s adult contemporary chart and received an Academy Award® nomination as well as three GRAMMY® awards. As you'll see, the jazzy theme, which evokes a panther slinking around, feels great under the fingers on the piano.

"The Pink Panther" owes its mysterious air to a preponderance of *chromatic* notes (those outside of the key, which is E minor) and to being in a low register. Note that both hands are written in the bass clef. When you're playing through the music, constantly scan ahead for *accidentals* (sharps and flats), so that your fingers don't get tripped up by them. It might also be a good idea to understand how the song's roadmap works before you start to play. When you get to the repeat before the coda, go back to play an octave higher (optional) than written until you see the indication *loco on repeat*. When you arrive at the repeat the second time, go to the sign and play the music as written until you see "To Coda," at which point you'll skip ahead to the coda. After you understand how everything works and begin to play along with the recording, be sure to lock in tight with the saxophone or flute to get that slinky feel down.

Signed, Sealed, Delivered I'm Yours *(page 62)*

Stevie Wonder was all of 20 years old when he recorded what would become one of his signature songs, "Signed, Sealed, Delivered I'm Yours," a number in which the narrator has gone and done something foolish and is now returning to his girl, begging for forgiveness. If you look at the songwriting credits, you'll see a composer who might be unfamiliar. Lula Mae Hardaway was Stevie Wonder's mother, and during his teenage years she sometimes acted as his writing partner. In fact, in 1970 she was nominated for a GRAMMY award for her work on "Signed, Sealed, Delivered I'm Yours." Although it's Little Stevie's vocal part that really makes the song, it also sounds great in a play-along piano context.

"Signed, Sealed, Delivered I'm Yours," is written here in the original key of F and kicks off with an arrangement of the sitar part (incidentally, an unusual instrument for an R&B song) heard on the original recording. This is another one of those songs where the groove comes from the bass line, so you might want to master the left-hand part before attempting to play everything together. Precise rhythmic placement is key here, so be sure that you can accurately feel the dotted eighth-sixteenth note rhythms, subdividing if needed. Also, dig the chromatic notes that occur here and there in the bass line, such as the E♭ in bar six. These pitches impart a funky flavor to the proceedings.

Sing (From Sesame Street) *(page 66)*

The children's television show *Sesame Street* has long been known for its hip music. One of the show's best-loved songs is "Sing," a jazzy song that the Carpenters covered in 1973, making it a big hit among general listening audiences. The song, which was written by *Sesame Street*'s staff songwriter, the late Joe Raposo, has since seen a surprisingly wide range of interpretations, from a hardcore version by the Dutch group Nakatomi to a country-tinged take by the Dixie Chicks. Our play-along version, though, stays pretty faithful to the original song.

Part of what makes "Sing" more sophisticated than typical music for children is its use of jazzy *seventh chords* such as E♭maj7 (E♭–G–B♭–D), Cm7 (C–E♭–G–B♭), Fm7 (F–A♭–C–E♭), and B♭7 (B♭–D–F–A♭). Before you attempt to play along with the CD, listen to the demo and follow along in the music, paying close attention to the sounds of these seventh chords. Then when you play the song, be sure to really relish these expressive chords. One more thing: Be sure to observe the articulation markings throughout. The *tenuto* marks (–) call for you to play the indicated notes in a slightly detached way, while the squiggly vertical line next to select chords calls for you to *roll* them from lowest note to highest.

Some Enchanted Evening *(page 70)*

South Pacific, the 1949 musical by Richard Rodgers and Oscar Hammerstein II, is widely considered one of the masterpieces of its genre. Like all great musicals, it spawned a number of popular standards, including "Younger Than Springtime" and "Some Enchanted Evening." The latter song has been recorded by everyone from Frank Sinatra to Barbra Streisand to the Temptations, and a listen to the demo track will show you why it's such a durable and enduring number.

To sound great when you play along with the CD on this track, you'll want to observe each expressive and tempo marking. For example, there are *crescendo* and *decrescendo* markings that appear throughout. Where you see either the text *cresc.* or a hairpin line with a closed beginning *(crescendo)*, gradually play more loudly. And where you see a hairpin line with an open beginning *(decrescendo)*, play gradually more quietly until you reach the point at which the lines close. In terms of tempo indications, *rit.*, or *ritard* directs you to slow down, while *a tempo* means for you to resume the original tempo. Observing details like these is what separates a merely acceptable play-along from an inspiring one.

Stand by Me (page 75)

One of the greatest songs in pop history, "Stand by Me" was almost never recorded. Ben E. King originally penned the number for his R&B vocal group the Drifters. They passed on it, though, and it wasn't until King needed some extra material for a solo session that he pulled out the song. Throughout the years King's 1960 original has inspired some great covers by John Lennon, U2, and, surprisingly, Cassius Clay (Muhammad Ali). And now you can play your own version with this handy play-along.

"Stand By Me" has one of the most common chord progressions in all of pop music: I-vi-IV-V (F–Dm–B♭–C). To learn the song, start with the left-hand bass line, which has the same basic rhythm the whole way through. Be sure to nail that syncopated note squarely on each beat 2, and as you play this part along with the CD, lock in tightly with the upright bass, the instrument also heard on the original recording. Next, work out the right-hand chords in the accompaniment. These appear in the introduction (first eight bars), and then as down-stemmed notes whenever the melody is present. Note that like the bass line, this accompaniment has a repetitive rhythm, with chord stabs in each measure on beat 2 and on the "and" of beat 3, so once you've got it down you'll be in great shape. Be sure to give the rests their full value, so that the music grooves. After you've got the bass and chord work sorted out, add the melody in the up-stemmed notes.

Sweet Caroline (page 78)

Sometime in the mid-1960s, Neil Diamond saw a magazine cover photo depicting a young Caroline Kennedy, and something about the image stuck with him. In 1969 the photo inspired Diamond's great song "Sweet Caroline," which would climb to #4 on the *Billboard* chart and sell more than a million singles. The song remains a crowd-pleaser, especially at sporting events. For instance, it's played in the middle of every eighth inning at Boston's Fenway Park. Our arrangement captures the song's infectious riffs and triumphant vocals in all their glory.

The left-hand part for "Sweet Caroline" is barebones and rather guitarlike, so imagine that you're picking on a six-string when you play along with the recording. And enjoy all the different textures in the music: single-note lines in the intro; then *power chords,* containing just roots and fifths in the verse; broken octaves in the pre-chorus (starting at the sign with the lyric "Hands,"); and a more rhythmically involved line that focuses on roots, thirds, and fifths in the chorus. Textural changes like these help differentiate sections and keep the music fresh and exciting for listeners.

Tennessee Waltz (page 84)

One of the great country-western songs, "Tennessee Waltz" was written by Redd Stewart and Pee Wee King in 1946 and became a huge hit four years later when it was recorded by Patti Page. The tune was so popular that in 1965 it became the official song of the state of Tennessee, and, earning a more curious distinction, in 1974 it became the biggest selling song that the country of Japan had ever seen. Play through our piano arrangement to find out for yourself why so many people have found this waltz so appealing.

"Tennessee Waltz" is arranged here in the key of G major. As indicated by the sign in parentheses next to the tempo marking, the music is played with a *swing* feel. Fundamental to jazz, this rhythmic feel causes notes ordinarily played straight to be played unevenly: a pair of consecutive eighth notes is rendered long-short, at approximately a ratio of two to one. Before you begin playing along with the CD, work on the swing feel: pick a single note and play it in a continuous stream of eighth notes, long-short, with a sort of bounce to the music, until you feel like you've got it down. Then, when you play the song, remember not just to play with the swing feel, but to waltz properly as well.

Time After Time (page 90)

Not to be confused with the Cyndi Lauper song of the same name, Sammy Cahn and Jule Styne's "Time After Time" was introduced by Frank Sinatra in the 1947 motion picture *It Happened in Brooklyn.* The tune quickly became a jazz standard and was recorded by heavyweights such as trumpeter Miles Davis and the singer Ella Fitzgerald. Our play-along version might not call for any improvisation, but its harmonies are jazzy for sure.

As most people know it, "Time After Time," arranged here in the key of C, starts after the first double bar, on the lyric "Time" (at about 1:04 on the play-along). Wherever you choose to start, our CD will have you playing along with a pretty fancy arrangement featuring a string section and harp. It could be a little tricky to follow the play-along, so be sure to lock in with the count-off before the music begins. To maintain the tempo in the first four bars, follow the bass, which plays a robust note on beat 1 of each bar. Beginning at bar five, get in sync with the violins, which take the melody here. Don't be distracted by the countermelodies played by the strings and harp — just home in again on the bass and this should help you keep your place in the music.

Watch What Happens (page 87)

Michel Legrand is one of France's most prolific composers, having written more than 200 scores for film and television. Although much of his film music is haunting, "Watch What Happens," a song from the score to 1964's *The Umbrellas of Cherbourg,* is in a cheerier style influenced by *bossa nova,* a type of Brazilian jazz that emerged several years before the movie was made. The song is a bit challenging, but rewarding to perform as a piano play-along.

"Watch What Happens" has some elements that might be rhythmically tricky. Be careful to keep the tempo steady as you move back and forth between 3/4 and 4/4 time in the first four bars. Take note of the quarter-note triplets throughout the music. If you need to review how to count and feel these, refer to the notes for "I'll Be There." The song can also be harmonically tricky. A lot of interesting things are going on here. For example, in bar 11, you'll see the same chord moving up by half steps for the progression E♭maj7–Emaj7–Fmaj7 and then back down. If you find that these chords are causing you to struggle to keep up with the play-along, turn off the CD and isolate any problematic spots until you can navigate them with ease.

Young at Heart (page 94)

"Young at Heart" is another golden song Frank Sinatra helped become a pop standard. In 1953 Sinatra was the first artist to record the song. It quickly became a hit, easily selling a million copies; a film made starring Sinatra at the time was even renamed "Young at Heart" and included the song during the opening and closing credits. Something about the song goes well with the silver screen and it has since been featured in movies like *It Could Happen to You* (1994) and *Space Cowboys* (2000), to name two. It's also been covered by performers as distinct in style as Shawn Colvin and Tom Waits. Our play-along version, though, sticks pretty closely to the 1953 original.

You'll find "Young at Heart" played here in the key of B♭ major. Listen to the demo and you'll hear that the melody is joyous and expressive. That's because the melody doesn't just move in little steps, it leaps around a bit, in a way that is almost childlike. For example, at the end of bar four, there's a jump of a *major sixth,* from F to D, then a descent of a *minor seventh,* from D to E, plus a descent of a *minor sixth,* from C to E, in the following bar. It's easy enough to play these intervals on the piano, but to make sure that you're really hearing them, try singing the song before you play it.

The Pink Panther

from THE PINK PANTHER
By Henry Mancini

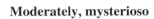

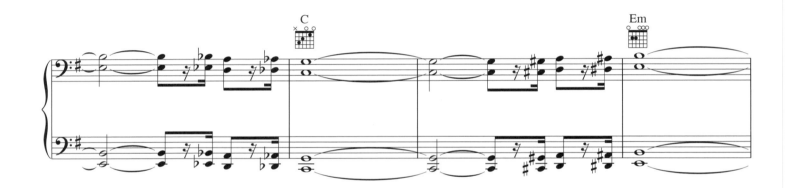

Signed, Sealed, Delivered I'm Yours

Words and Music by Stevie Wonder, Syreeta Wright,
Lee Garrett and Lula Mae Hardaway

Like a fool I went and stayed ___ too long. ___
Then that time I went and said ___ good - bye. ___
Seen a lot of things in this ___ old world. ___
Ooh - wee babe, you set my world ___ on fire. ___

Now I'm won - d'rin' if ___ your love's still strong. ___
Now I'm back ___ and not ___ a - shamed to cry. ___
When I touched ___ them they ___ did noth - ing, girl. ___
That's why I know you're my one and on - ly de - sire. ___

Oo   ba -

Sing

from SESAME STREET
Words and Music by Joe Raposo

Some Enchanted Evening

from SOUTH PACIFIC
Lyrics by Oscar Hammerstein II
Music by Richard Rodgers

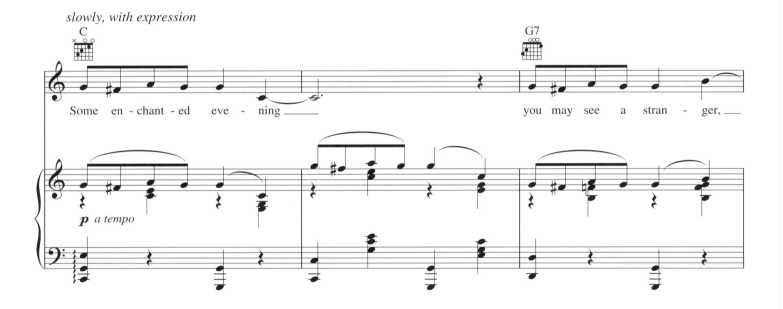

Stand By Me

Words and Music by Jerry Leiber,
Mike Stoller and Ben E. King

Sweet Caroline

Words and Music by Neil Diamond

Where it be - gan, ___

I can't be - gin to know - in', but then I

And when I hurt, ___ hurt - in' runs off my shoul - ders.

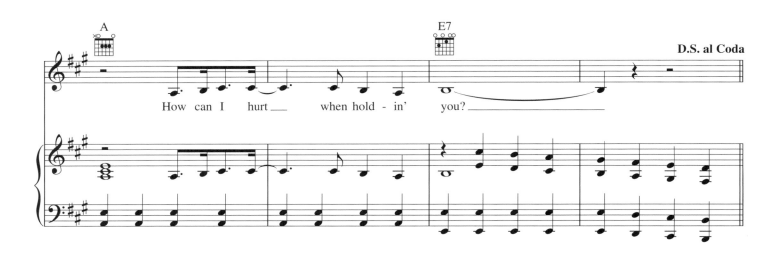

How can I hurt ___ when hold - in' you? _____

D.S. al Coda

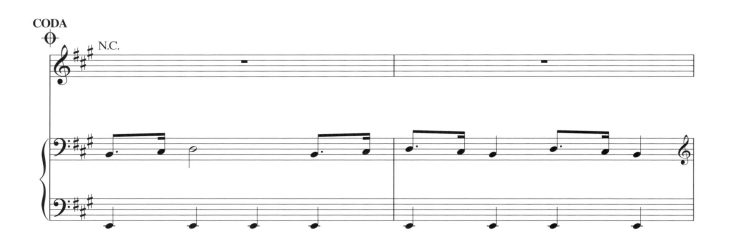

CODA

N.C.

Tennessee Waltz

Words and Music by Redd Stewart and Pee Wee King

Watch What Happens

from THE UMBRELLAS OF CHERBOURG
Music by Michel Legrand
Original French Text by Jacques Demy
English Lyrics by Norman Gimbel

Time After Time

from the Metro-Goldwyn-Mayer Picture IT HAPPENED IN BROOKLYN
Words by Sammy Cahn
Music by Jule Styne

Young at Heart

from YOUNG AT HEART
Words by Carolyn Leigh
Music by Johnny Richards